More Deep End of the Pool

Another collection of dreamy, surreal imagery and starkly honest
commentary on the waters in which we all swim.

Published by:

Indie Arts Productions
PO Box 1052
Beaverton, OR 97075
www.deependofthepool.com

ISBN-10:098501881X
ISBN-13:978-0-9850188-1-8

Printed by CreateSpace.

Introduction

More Deep End of the Pool is another collection of 35 surreal, dreamy imagery and starkly honest commentary on the waters in which we all swim. This exploration of the poetic universe is a journey within a journey and a dream within a dream. Dive into the emerging, morphing universe to discover a fresh view of ordinary reality.

Tuckle your timmy with writings that are humorous and personal insights on stuff about booting the inner critic, waking up and bad poetry. They are paired with colorful, playful digital collages in postcard format to illustrate the silly, profound and mystical experiences of life.

A koan is an example of a paradox that transcends reason and logic while confounding the intellect. "What is the sound of one hand clapping?" is an example of a Zen koan. This can allow a different level of understanding to dawn by transcending the paradox.

Because of the unexpected combination of elements in these collages, they have been called visual koans. Finding the startling and entangled relationships between random elements requires a stretch of the imagination and rewards with a thrill when a connection is made.

> "By blending and layering rich and unrelated images, I explore the strange world of the unified field of quantum physics, where timelessness and the mysterious entanglement of sub-atomic particles contain the potential for unlimited possibilities." -- Karen Landey

Welcome to **More Deep End of the Pool**.

Buffalo

POST CARD

THIS SPACE FOR ADDRESS ONLY

buf·fa·lo   (bŭf'ə-lō')

Noun
1. The North American bison
2. A city in New York

Verb
1. To intimidate, as by a display of confidence
2. To deceive; hoodwink

Carte Postale

More Deep End of the Pool

Buffalo

Caution Falling Rain

POST CARD

THIS SPACE FOR ADDRESS ONLY

Terminal Velocity

The waiting is the hardest part. She can't allow
regrets or her world would fold in on itself.

Carte Postale

More Deep End of the Pool

Caution Falling Rain

Dabbling Forbidden

POST CARD
THIS SPACE FOR ADDRESS ONLY

Butch Cassidy's Mug Shot

Thought I would share some of my favorite
spoonerisms. I actually said these!

Tuckle your timmy (tickle your tummy.)
    I said this to my cat.
Spits and farts (fits and starts.)
    I said this at a very important meeting.
Crooks and nannies (nooks and crannies.)
    I said this to myself.

Carte Postale

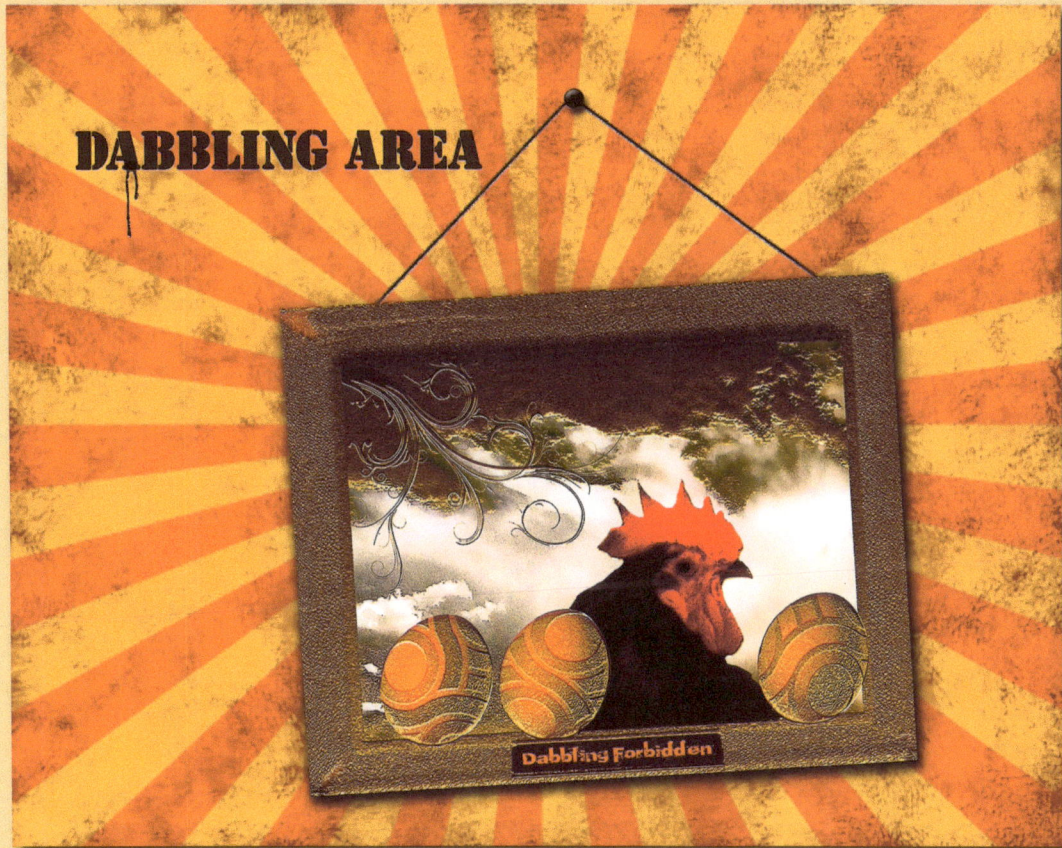

Dabbling Forbidden

Dance at Dawn

POST CARD

THIS SPACE FOR ADDRESS ONLY

Destination Unknown

It does no good to wonder where I am going, only that I will arrive at my destination. Destiny and destination originate from the same Latin word, destinare; to choose that which is firmly determined by fate.

If destiny is the result of the choices I make, it takes courage to know that my journey is discovering my destination, one step at a time.

Carte Postale

More Deep End of the Pool

Dance at Dawn

Diva Diva

POST CARD

THIS SPACE FOR ADDRESS ONLY

I have been piecing together my personal mythology by paying attention to the images, words and thoughts that recur over and over again. They point in the direction of understanding what makes me who I am as I journey on my path of self-revelation. The easiest way for me to do this is to use mixed media collage to allow my subconscious free rein to play so these images and insights will come to the surface where I can use them.

Carte Postale

More Deep End of the Pool

Diva Diva

Dream Walker

POST CARD

THIS SPACE FOR ADDRESS ONLY

Address Unknown

I explore the world of mystical visions through the eyes of a dream walker or lucid dreamer who travels through dimensions while remaining conscious of its illusory nature. They navigate surreal landscapes that intersect with other realities on their mystical journey.

Carte Postale

More Deep End of the Pool

Dream Walker

First Class Passenger

POST CARD

THIS SPACE FOR ADDRESS ONLY

I am sorry to hear you sound so sad. I think you
may be overly tired and stressed? The only thing
I really worry about is that you will lose your heart.
Its OK to drift around, you will find a shore eventually.

Keeping the light on...

Carte Postale

First Class Passenger

Fishing License

POST CARD

THIS SPACE FOR ADDRESS ONLY

I forget what it's like to be ice as the warmth of the sun
melts crystallized edges, following the flow of least
resistance. I know eventually I'll return to mist but
until then, I run free and easy.

Carte Postale

More Deep End of the Pool

Fishing License

Flying Lessons

POST CARD

THIS SPACE FOR ADDRESS ONLY

No Return

I was unaware until I saw a program on TV, that caterpillars completely liquefy inside their cocoons. There is no turning back from being half liquid and saying, "Wait, I changed my mind!"

What would you change into if you could be anything you wanted? Would you be willing to undergo a complete transformation to attain your desires?

Carte Postale

Flying Lessons

Freeze Frame

POST CARD

THIS SPACE FOR ADDRESS ONLY

The natural world is poignantly beautiful in its symmetry and natural rhythm.

Carte Postale

More Deep End of the Pool

Freeze Frame

23

Grace

POST CARD
THIS SPACE FOR ADDRESS ONLY

TRAVEL
ANYWHERE EVERYWHERE

I am over letting pain having it's way with me. I shift my focus to what makes me feel happy, healthy, optimistic. By doing so, I create an energy field that attracts like energy.

It doesn't take any more effort to think positive thoughts rather than pessimistic thoughts. It means I have to be aware of what I am thinking and feeling and shift when I catch myself thinking negatively.

Carte Postale

More Deep End of the Pool

Grace

I Was There

POST CARD

THIS SPACE FOR ADDRESS ONLY

A memento is a reminder of the past; a keepsake. Each remembrance contains a holographic memory full of the sights, sounds, tastes, smells and sensations of that experience. Bring all of its depth and intensity into the present moment stripped of its past association to explore the new places it takes you.

Carte Postale

More Deep End of the Pool

I Was There

Looking In

POST CARD

THIS SPACE FOR ADDRESS ONLY

My art deals a lot with intimacy; not the physical kind, but the soul to soul kind. Opening my heart completely to a stranger while walking past on the street; intimacy with a memory that only I can remember; intimacy with a friend while laughing hysterically over some private joke. My art is my soul turned inside out for the whole world to see.

Carte Postale

Looking In

Luscious

POST CARD

THIS SPACE FOR ADDRESS ONLY

SPOLETO
VMBRIA

The path of least resistance is the key to knowing
that I am on the road to finding the work that is most
creative and rewarding. Though the journey may take
me through some strange territory, I enjoy the scenery
moment by moment.

Carte Postale

More Deep End of the Pool

Luscious

Open Mind

POST CARD

THIS SPACE FOR ADDRESS ONLY

Rush

So am I. Nuts. That is.
Where did that insane laughter come from?
A little mad. I hate it when people squander opportunities.
Like you did today. Not sure why I care.
I just made you read (bad) poetry.
So there.

Carte Postale

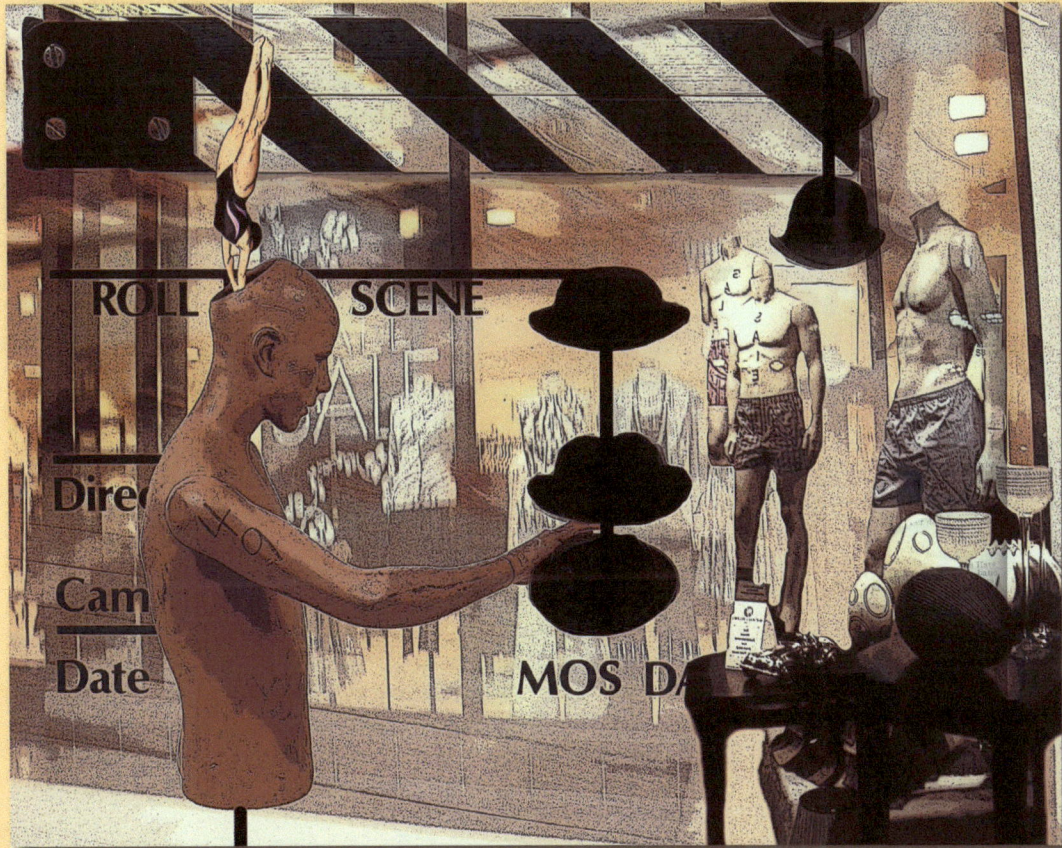

Open Mind

Outpost

POST CARD

THIS SPACE FOR ADDRESS ONLY

Art is my first life line.

Phone a friend is my second.

Ask the The Google is my third.

Carte Postale

More Deep End of the Pool

Outpost

Passing Through

POST CARD

THIS SPACE FOR ADDRESS ONLY

As long as I'm invisible, no one asks anything of me or can see how much pain I'm really in.

Being visible means that everyone can see when I'm hurting but also when I'm fully present, feeling radiant.

I think its worth the risk.

Carte Postale

More Deep End of the Pool

Passing Through

Photo Shoot

POST CARD

THIS SPACE FOR ADDRESS ONLY

I am a complex little bean. Not a jelly bean, nor a common bean
and especially not a kidney bean which is toxic unless thoroughly
cooked. Maybe a velvet bean or a winged bean. Yes! I am a
winged bean.

Maybe you are a moth bean, a black turtle bean, a hyacinth bean,
a black-eye pea or a jack bean. Somthing more exotic? How about
a Valentine bean, a Domino bean, a Robust bean, a Maverick bean
or a Pinto Horse bean. Maybe you are a winged bean too, or one
that has yet to be discovered...

Carte Postale

Photo Shoot

Posed

POST CARD
THIS SPACE FOR ADDRESS ONLY

The flutter of found wings inside the dream
reminds me I am not asleep.

Carte Postale

More Deep End of the Pool

Posed

Promenade

POST CARD
THIS SPACE FOR ADDRESS ONLY

Sometimes I run into obstacles that stop me in my tracks.
If these roadblocks are met with courage and creativity,
I can find a solution that not only moves me forward, but
opens a door to a possibility I had not previously considered.
It becomes a better direction than the one in which I was
initially headed.

Carte Postale

More Deep End of the Pool

Promenade

Raw Silk

POST CARD
THIS SPACE FOR ADDRESS ONLY

There is an unseen light that surrounds each person that
draws experiences into its sphere according to its quality
and brilliance.

Carte Postale

Raw Silk

Safari

POST CARD

THIS SPACE FOR ADDRESS ONLY

ROYAL HOTEL
BANGKOK

The fragile boundary meant to keep the universes parallel
is breached by a dream of starlight. The traveler discovers
an altered vision and a fresh view of ordinary reality.

Carte Postale

More Deep End of the Pool

Safari

Secret Grove

POST CARD

THIS SPACE FOR ADDRESS ONLY

The fleeting moment contrasts with the timelessness of ancient mysteries. From these gifts of our ancestors we wonder where we came from, why we are here and feel a sense of connection to the past, present and future.

"When you look into an abyss, the abyss also looks into you."
   --Friedrich Nietzsche

Carte Postale

More Deep End of the Pool

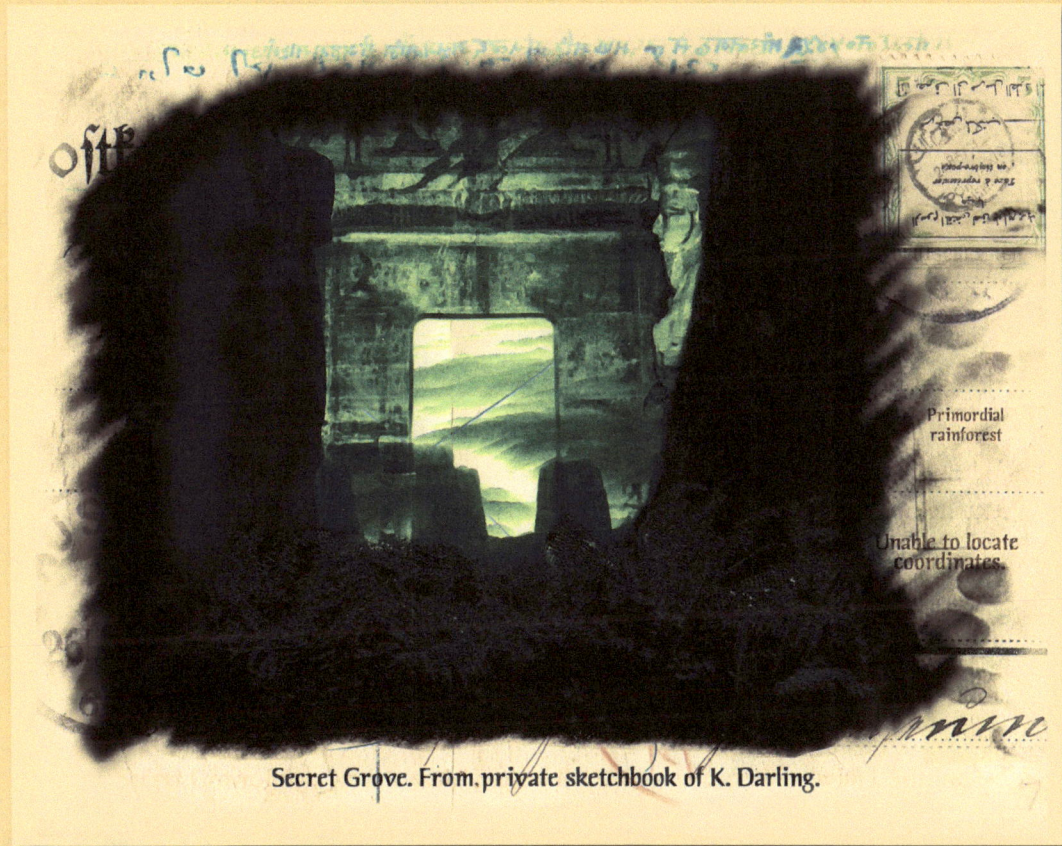

Secret Grove. From private sketchbook of K. Darling.

Secret Grove

Sightseeing Tours

POST CARD

THIS SPACE FOR ADDRESS ONLY

LA·SPARTANA

INTERNATIONAL MAIL

Essential Hong Kong Cantonese (remembered after almost 40 years.)

Jo San! ~ Good Morning!

Yao loke! ~ Stop here!
(Say loudly from the back of the bus when you need to get off NOW!)

Yum Sing! Yum Joy! ~ Drinking toasts

M'goi mi don ~ Waiter, my check
(Accompanied by a writing-on-paper mime)

No!: No! (say to mafia guy who wants to buy your body for an hour.)

Carte Postale

More Deep End of the Pool

Sightseeing Tours

Silent Witness

POST CARD

THIS SPACE FOR ADDRESS ONLY

I believe we each have a silent witness that is the space in which thoughts exist and where the viewer becomes aware of herself.

Fragile thoughts are caught within the neural network of the brain. Memories become colored by repetitive recreation in the imagination. The silent observer bears witness to them all without judgment.

Carte Postale

More Deep End of the Pool

Silent Witness

Still Life with Roadster

POST CARD

THIS SPACE FOR ADDRESS ONLY

What is the creative process and how can you wrap yourself in it? The answer is to play, play, play. You can't afford not to play! You add so much richness to your life when you allow yourself to drop into the moment, the creative zone, where ideas have a chance to get your attention.

Once you open the door to creativity, you will find yourself attracting ideas. When you have made yourself a magnet for ideas, be receptive and willing to listen. Always have paper and pencil nearby to capture them.

Carte Postale

Still Life With Roadster

Sunset

POST CARD

THIS SPACE FOR ADDRESS ONLY

In the magical space between sunlight and starlight, I search
for the one who will call me home at last. The wandering will
cease and my heart, tried by fire, will be cooled by rain.

I will find the doorway to timelessness.

Carte Postale

More Deep End of the Pool

Sunset

57

Sweeties

POST CARD

THIS SPACE FOR ADDRESS ONLY

THE TANGO
Two Step

I love the idea of timeless joy, making it independent of whatever happens in my life day to day. I'm waking up to the heart of what makes me feel effortless, buoyant, effervescent, candid.

Carte Postale

More Deep End of the Pool

Sweeties

Tattoo Parlor

POST CARD

THIS SPACE FOR ADDRESS ONLY

Wanna come to the tattoo parlor with me?
Get a nice scowly face on your arm.
That way, you don't have to wear one on your face!

Carte Postale

More Deep End of the Pool

Tattoo Parlor

Temple Ruins

POST CARD

THIS SPACE FOR ADDRESS ONLY

RIGOLETTO

My inner critical editor needs to be booted. Honestly, I don't know how it got so freaking entrenched. Now that I am determined to wake up, it seems to be getting more devious! Maybe just ignoring it will make it go away. Maybe making friends with my enemy will make it an ally.

Carte Postale

More Deep End of the Pool

Temple Ruins

The Last Tango

POST CARD

THIS SPACE FOR ADDRESS ONLY

You are like a room that feels comfy and
familiar and full of joy when the door is open.

Carte Postale

More Deep End of the Pool

The Last Tango

The Roller Coaster

POST CARD

THIS SPACE FOR ADDRESS ONLY

TWO
BUTTERFLIES

INSPECTED
BY
HARA YUSHUTSUTEN
FOR
TATA SONS & CO

I think entering the realm of deep relationship is the revealing of my heart and the rendering of tears stored there, both happy and sad.

They fall upon the dry earth of my mind and from them springs the knowledge that I will be healed and made whole through the sacrifice of my fear.

Carte Postale

More Deep End of the Pool

Ride at your own risk

The Roller Coaster

Trophies

POST CARD

THIS SPACE FOR ADDRESS ONLY

We lose our humanity when we give in to fear.

I don't mean the real fear of imminent danger; I mean the
ignorant fear we project onto others in unreasoned hate
and prejudice.

Carte Postale

Trophies

Unique Cart

POST CARD

THIS SPACE FOR ADDRESS ONLY

We need to filter what we say and not just blurt out raw data. I am guilty of doing that and more than once have said, "Did I just say that out loud?"

Carte Postale

Unique Cart

Wise Ones

POST CARD

THIS SPACE FOR ADDRESS ONLY

SPEAKER

This is the Operator speaking. In order to
continue this conversation, please remove one
of your swarming ideas from your In Box and put
it in your Out Box. Describe with your right brain.

Carte Postale

More Deep End of the Pool

Wise Ones

Acknowledgements

Images used in the digital collages are from the artist's photos and artwork, found ephemera, public domain photos and copyright-free sources.

Thank you to my family and friends who have supported me through the years.

Special thanks to my ghosty friend, Boo.

About the Artist

Karen Landey is an award-winning collage artist and indie video producer. She traveled wildly before finding a home in the Pacific Northwest. She loves walking in the clouds and asking questions that have no answers.

Each of her collages tells a story that conveys her sense of humor. By playing with alternative meanings of cliché expressions, she gives them surprising and unique twists.

> "I explore the deep and mysterious realms of dreams and visions by blending and layering rich and unrelated images. These surreal and mystical landscapes are rich worlds in which to tell stories. By being present in the moment I allow the creative and intuitive self to find new depths and insights.

> "The interface between the unified field of quantum physics and the spiritual and mystical realms continues to intrigue me. This radiant edge inspires me to find ways to bring my vision through my artwork and into the world."

She released ten DVD's including nine issues of **INDIE ARTS: The DVD Magazine,** a cutting edge format featuring interviews with over 60 artists. Her tenth DVD release, **Entangled: Video Art by Karen Landey** includes 14 of her short films which screened in film festivals in the U.S. and internationally.

www.ingramcontent.com/pod-product-compliance
Lightning Source LLC
Chambersburg PA
CBHW060821270326
41931CB00002B/45